FROM THE PORCH SWING

From The Porch Swing

My Life, My Dreams and Other Things

Poems By

MARY JANE HALEY

iUniverse, Inc.
Bloomington

From The Porch Swing
My Life, My Dreams and Other Things

iUniverse books may be ordered through booksellers or by contacting:

iUniverse
1663 Liberty Drive
Bloomington, IN 47403
www.iuniverse.com
1-800-Authors (1-800-288-4677)

ISBN: 978-1-4759-6722-7 (sc)
ISBN: 978-1-4759-6723-4 (e)

Library of Congress Control Number: 2013900052

Printed in the United States of America

iUniverse rev. date: 1/8/2013

My parents, Hazel and Lee Griffith
(About 1937)

For my parents, Hazel and Lee Griffith, and my grandparents, Ellen and Johnny Griffith and Lucy and Gordon Fitzwater, with love and appreciation. They made my childhood and indeed, my whole life, beautiful and full.

Table of Contents

Memories and Reflections

*My brother, David Griffith (left), and my cousin, John Poston
Fishing in the Birch River in West Virginia (about 1946)*

My sister June with Old Blue, the fox hound
(about 1929)

The Christmas I Was Five

The apple trees were glistening in the early light of dawn
and the snow made fairy castles on the lawn.

Down the lane came Papa with the horses and the sleigh,
as the church bells were all ringing in the day.

For it was winter in the mountains with snow drifts all around
and still the shining snowflakes drifted down.

I stood watching through the window and my little
      candle flame
turned the tiny snowflakes into diamonds on the pane.

Tomorrow would be Christmas day and Papa brought the tree.
I knew tonight Kris Kringle would bring Christmas gifts
      for me.

I could hear the sleigh bells tinkling and could smell the
      pumpkin pies.
I could see the Christmas spirit in my mother's loving eyes.

Now I watch the snowflakes and that Christmas comes alive.
I shall not forget a moment of the Christmas I was five.

Echoes of Yesterday

I returned to the scene of my childhood today
on the Magothy River down by the bay,
where we sailed in the sun every summer day
before we grew up and drifted away.

The gentle waves whispered "stay, won't you stay,"
and my heart heard the echoes of yesterday.

The dock was deserted, no ships on the bay,
but seagulls wheeled in the sky far away.
I sat alone thinking of sailing all day,
and remembering friends now far, far away.

The gentle waves whispered "stay, won't you stay,"
and my heart heard the echoes of yesterday.

In the last rays of sun, a sail caught the light
like wings of a seagull rising in flight.
Was it fantasy then as it faded from sight,
That I heard my name on the wind of the night?

While the gentle waves whispered "stay, won't you stay,"
my heart heard the echoes of yesterday.

Sea Wind

Soft is the wind from off the sea
    and sweet the salt-brine flavor.
Soft is its touch upon my cheek
    as if my warmth to savor
as we once touched on such a day
    when winds were soft and warm
and life was sweet with new-found love:
    the lull before the storm;
before the storm which battered love
    and swept away all feeling,
leaving us on foreign paths
    to seek our own heart's healing.

Now on another sun-swept beach
    with wind soft from the sea,
the memory of that first sweet love
    creeps softly back to me.
As I remember tender love,
    and feel again the pain,
I know that if I could go back
    I'd want it all again.
For soft is the wind from off the sea
    and sweet its salt-brine flavor,
fraught with the essence of the past
    and memories sweet to savor.

Homesick

I get homesick for those West Virginia hills.
Sometimes it makes me feel so blue!
But that old time saying that you can't go home again
turns out to be completely true.

There was a time when I went back
and they'd all come out to meet me at the door.
But now the house is just an empty shell
and there's no one there to greet me any more.

The barn is empty and the loft is full of birds.
I can look right through the house and see the sky.
But I can almost see my Mama and my Daddy
as I sit down on the porch and start to cry.

I look around and see no rows of corn.
The apple trees and flowers are all gone.
It's true there is no house where I was born
but in my heart of hearts it will live on.

*Grandpa and Grandma's House in West Virginia where
I lived as a teenager after my grandparents had passed
away. I was born in a beautiful log cabin that Daddy
built on the hill overlooking both this house and my other
grandparents' house. (This one was built around 1904.)*

The House Where I Was Born

Oh, little house among the trees
    where I once played at Mama's knees
    and ran as free as a mountain breeze.
    Oh, sweet, enduring memories!

I need but close my weary eyes
    to see again that paradise
    where West Virginia mountains rise
    to meet the blue of summer skies.

I see the house where I was born
    neglected now and all forlorn
    old and dark, all beauty shorn,
    Oh, little house where I was born!

The Peace of Country Roads

When a boy walks barefoot down a dusty country road,
    (a joy, of course, not everyone has sought),
small puffs of dust rise up between his toes,
    and absorb beyond the need for conscious thought.

He has no need to notice beauty all around him
    nor note the morning glories in the corn:
He is a boy at one with nature and at peace,
    feeling, more than seeing country morn.

The peace of country roads and dusty lanes,
    as much a part of boy as skin and bone
will live within his soul through time and space
    where often times a man must walk alone.

And when he tires of walking foreign streets
    he'll seek the surest source of peace he knows:
he'll walk again the quiet country roads
    and feel once more the dust between his toes

Dreaming in the Garden

In my garden there are flowers just like Grandma used to grow.
They bloom in great profusion, just like dancers in a show.
Their pretty heads are tossed by every gentle breeze
that comes to dance and play among their gently swaying leaves.

There are Roses and Begonias, Impatience and Sweet Peas;
Snap Dragons and Petunias and Rose of Sharon trees.
There are Delphinium and Cosmos, Portulaca and Old Maids;
Bachelor's Buttons and Sweet Williams forever on parade.

Lying in my hammock, I watch the Flags unfurl.
then close my eyes and dream that I am still a little girl,
Standing in the garden with Grandma's hand in mine,
breathing in the perfume of the honeysuckle vine.

Great Uncle Fred, Grandpa Griffith, Grandma Griffith and my brother David. About 1936.

A Summer Day

Down in the valley where the green grass grows
    and Blue Bells bloom in the sun,
an old man sits 'neath the old Oak tree
    on the banks of Willow Run.

He dreams of days of a youth long gone
    and waits for the fish to bite,
but a small boy wades in the rippling stream
    and the fish stay out of sight.

It doesn't matter if the fish don't bite
    for its cool on the banks of the creek,
the small boy knows where the crawdads hide
    and the bees sing the old man to sleep.

Creek Wading

Moss grows thick on dark, wet stones
    and roots protrude like gnarled bones.

A swallow sings in the old birch tree
    and sun-warmed berries hang temptingly

A breeze runs by on velvet feet,
    summer warm, perfumed and sweet.

A squirrel eats nuts in a nearby tree
    while dog sleeps on, obliviously.

Cool water washes over dirty bare toes.
    Oh, what joy a small boy knows!

Through The Old Man's Eyes

The old man smiled and said he thought the world
    a lovely place to be
and through his words I saw what he could see:

A drop of dew for one brief shining moment
    shimmers in the sun
and then is gone though day has just begun;

A graceful deer so still at forest's edge,
    Suspended in his flight,
and almost hidden in the dappled light;

A bird somewhere among the apple trees,
    his song a joyful prayer
for all the world to hear and share;

A child who runs and jumps in pure delight,
    his happiness outrageous
and his laughter quite contagious.

The old man smiled and said he thought the world
    a lovely place to be
and now I must confess: I quite agree!

My father, Lee Griffith (The Old Man of the Mountains), with Oscar the duck

The Old Man of the Mountains

Down in West Virginia where the hills rise green and steep
    the old man of the mountains
      now sleeps that long, long sleep.

He loved to hear the music of the thrush and whip-poor-will,
    and surely as they sing each day
      the old man hears them still.

He heard his name upon the wind and music in the streams
    and where the stream meets mountain trail,
      he surely sits and dreams.

Now when I walk by the old bear rock or pass the big bee tree,
    or sit beside a mountain stream,
      I know he's there with me.

Green Mountains

What ancient power do these green mountains have
    that I am ever drawn
to walk cool paths beneath the towering oaks
    where columbine and mountain laurel cling
and cliffs adorned with rusty, blue-green moss
    rise ponderous, cold and still
beside the rushing, laughing mountain streams
    while through the rustling leaves the soft winds sing.

The desert has a beauty of its own
    where earth and sky are one.
Cactus flow'rs splash red against the earth
    and blue vistas stretch as far as one can see.
Yet far away there is another world
    where towering oaks reach up and up and up
to join the misty sky with cool, green earth.

    What power is there that will not set me free?

Elegy of a Mountain Child

There is a cabin on a hill,
now stark and bare and deathly still
where I once lived, a mountain child,
gentle born and forest wild.

Oh, would that I could stand once more
beside that humble cabin door
and watch old moon reveal his face
and turn the trees to Queen Anne's lace;

And hear my mother singing soft,
the cattle lowing in the croft;
and in the woods familiar sounds
of bird and beast on daily rounds.

Then would I find myself again,
a ragged waif with shaggy mane
but happy in that paradise
where West Virginia mountains rise

To meet the stars in summer skies,
reducing man to trifling size;
and then transformed by winter snow,
a fairy land where day dreams grow.

Austere and dark those ancient hills,
yet water flows in sparkling rills
from cliffs laid bare by ice-age slides
on glacier tortured mountain sides.

Moonbeams dance upon the scree
beneath a knobby old pine tree
and wild, tenacious laurel clings
beside mysterious fairy rings.

It's here my shade will come at last
to meet the echoes of my past;
to sit beside some mountain stream
and dream that old familiar dream

Of a lonely cabin on a hill
once warm with love, now deathly still,
where I once lived, a mountain child,
gentle born and forest wild.

My father, Lee Griffith (left) at the entrance to the drift mine where he worked. He was showing a friend from the city the coal mines.

Summer Love Remembered

Birdsong
and old shade tree,
the buzzing of a jarfly;
all of these are dear to me,
awakening a memory
of lovely days gone by . . . gone by.

Sunshine
and lemon tea,
a fragment of a song;
all of these bring back to me
days beside a summer sea.
Have winters always been so long . . . so long?

Summer rain
and cornflowers blue,
the fragrance of a salty sea;
all of these are lovely too,
reminding me of days with you.
Will summer bring you to the sea . . . and me?

Got to Hear Them Wheels

Ol' Bowlegs was a coal mine man.
It was all he ever knew.
He broke his back a loadin' coal
Because he wanted to.

Got to hear them wheels, rollin', rollin',
Got to hear them wheels.

Sometimes I'd ask ol' Bowlegs,
"What is it makes you stay""
Ol' Bowlegs he'd just grin at me
And this is what he'd say.

Got to hear them wheels, rollin', rollin',
Got to hear them wheels.

"I know it's dark and it ain't too safe
and there ain't much room for walkin',
but I guess I'll keep on loadin' coal
just to hear them wheels a talkin'.

Got to hear them wheels, rollin', rollin',
Got to hear them wheels.

And if that slate should fall on me
and if perchance I die,
bury my bones by the old drift mine
and roll them wheels on by.

Got to hear them wheels, rollin', rollin',
Got to hear them wheels.

*Note: This poem is about a real person, "Bowlegs" Clendenin,
who worked for my father in the coal mines.*

A Summer of Reminders

Early morning shadows on dew-wet grass
    or a cornflower blossom among the weeds
can bring me poignant memories of home
    and deep, cool woods full of flowers
and birds.

My heart aches to go home again and be
    a child running free through fields of corn
or in the orchards picking peaches and pears
    or going to the barn on a cold winter morning
to gather eggs.

A single rose in the grocery store cooler
    can make me long for country gardens,
full of brilliant color and redolent with sage;
    and shady country lanes leading nowhere
in particular.

A street vendor sells vegetables and fruit
    and suddenly I remember fresh tomatoes
still warm from the morning sun,
    corn on the cob and hot homemade biscuits
dripping with butter.

Early morning shadows on wet green grass
    after a night of warm summer rain
make my heart ache and suddenly I long
    for deep, cool woods full of flowers
and birds.

A Poor Mountain Boy

He once was a poor boy who lived in the mountains;
 a poor mountain boy who had never done wrong.
His clothes were all ragged, his shoes didn't fit him
 but he plucked a guitar and sang a good song.

The life of the city called out to his spirit.
 He wanted to go where the lights were so bright;
where the girls wore red lipstick and soft satin dresses
 and danced to loud music for most of the night.

So he plucked his guitar and saved all his money,
 then kissed his old mother and father goodbye.
He left his sweet Susie a cryin' and moanin'.
 She thought in the city he surely would die.

Well he went to the city and made a small fortune
 a pluckin' his guitar and singin' his songs.
But he shouldn't have left his sweet little Susie
 a cryin' and moanin' for now she is gone.

Oh, why did he leave his life as a poor boy?
 Why did he leave his Susie so sweet?
Now all he has left are the lights of the city
 And the red-lipstick smiles of the girls on the street.

A Mother's Love

The three of us – me, my brother, David and my sister, June (about 1936)

A Mother's Love

A mother holds a child close in her arms,
    flesh of her flesh, heart of her heart,
and no matter how he grows
    or where he goes,
in her mind and soul, they are never far apart.

The child will go his own way all too soon,
    go from her arms to some far place
but no matter what he tries,
    or where he flies,
in her heart and soul forever lives his face.

A mother holds a child close within her love;
    flesh of her flesh, part of her heart,
and no matter what, he yearns,
    and always he returns,
for in their minds and souls they are never far apart.

Prayer for My Son

If there be sunshine, let my son live in it.
If there be joy, let him know it in full.
Let his happiness be like sunshine, infinite,
Let his joy live in him forever like a jewel.
For my son has given happiness and joy.
He has known trouble and won and lives.
My son has made me proud, this man, this boy.
Let him know his true worth and receive as he gives.

My Son

My son, my son –
    I always knew you would grow up and go your way,
    but not so soon! You were a baby in my arms just yesterday!

I look at you –
    And I still see that sweet, blond baby playing in the sand;
    the round, rosy cheeks, the dimpled baby hands.

But I know it's true –
    A baby becomes a man and follows his own destiny
    fulfilling dreams, the choice of pathways many.

My son, my son –
    I watch your strong hands as they pluck the strings
    of your guitar
    and I know that you will reach the heights, will land upon a star.

And yet, a mother cries –
    For sons who once were babies playing in the sand
    with sunburned cheeks and chubby legs, suntanned.

But you must go now –
    Out into the world according to God's plan.
    you are grown and I am proud – my baby is a man.

Letting Go

The hardest thing is letting go
as children grow.
They're individuals you know.
But it's very hard to let them go.

The hardest thing is letting go
as children grow.
You love your little babies so.
But you must be strong and let them go.

You always know that this is so
as children grow:
The hardest thing is letting go . . .
Is letting go.

Santa Doesn't Come Here Anymore

Santa doesn't come here anymore,
though the tree stands shining by the door.
The children are all grown and gone away
and I face a long and lonely Christmas day.

Santa doesn't come here anymore.
At least that's what I thought before
I heard the doorbell ring and ran to see
My children home for Christmas day with me.

For My Son

God made you, my son, exceedingly fair.
An angel kissed your cheek and left a dimple there.
Then God put a light in your eyes with care,
And just for good measure, put curls in your hair.

God, of course, knew what a boy he was making.
He knew that the world could be yours for the taking.
But, oh my son, my heart is breaking
for all the good things of this world you're forsaking.

So bring out the dimples and polish that smile,
for God only gives us a little while
to accomplish our goals, for life is a trial
and I know, my son, you can do it with style.

Wake up your ambition and open your mind.
If only you try I know you will find
you can be a success of a wonderful kind,
but you must leave your troublesome friends far behind.

A Day By The Sea

Soft is the wind and clean and free
    that whispers in from out to sea
to cool the sand beneath my feet
    and soothe my soul with sea air sweet.

Warm is the sun upon my face
    endowing now with perfect grace
the wet sand castle we have made,
    the child and I, with pail and spade.

For just this moment time stands still
    and then moves on against my will.
Long evening shadows soon intrude.
    It's almost done, this interlude.

And yet we linger for a while –
    Naught matters now but grandchild's smile,
warm as the sun upon the sand,
    bright as the seashell in her hand.

And soft is the wind and clean and free
    that whispers in from o'er the sea
so wind and sea and I can meet
    for one more hour with child so sweet.

Child Of My Child

The morning sun is caught within the halo of her hair,
    as golden as the flower in her hand,
and the fountain of her laughter bubbles up as light as air
    as she runs on chubby legs across the sand.

She turns to see if Grandma is still there
    and the smile upon her face is like the sun.
Light of my life, oh, child so fair,
    she would bring joy and love to anyone.

My heart is full of love and I am back in time
    with another little girl I love so much;
for this is the child of my child, all grown up
    the child whose heart I can no longer touch.

Then my daughter comes to take her baby home:
    my little grandchild, how my heart aches when I see
you wave goodbye and go, your hand in hers,
    but I know that this is just as it should be.

Moon Child

When the earth has gone full circle
and no longer casts her shadow on the moon;
when everything is washed in moon's white light,
the full moon seems to call you with some strange pied-piper's tune,
and lures you out on some unearthly flight.

She leads you in the dancing
in the fountain in the square
where you can hear her silent wolf-moon song,
then casts her strange exotic spell with moonbeams in your hair
and you are one with moon's enchanted throng.

The moon is more your mother
than the one who gave you birth.
They think you strange who do not hear her call,
but when she bares her shining face your mother feels her spell
and cannot think her daughter strange at all.

Heartaches

My painting, Lonesome Landscape

All my children. Left to right: Billy, Jimmy, Kelli, Joey, Erin and Kathy.

Note: Angels in the Snow was written for Kathy whom we lost after open heart surgery when she was seven years old. Joe died from cancer in 2000 when he was 36 years old. As yet I have not had the courage to write a poem for Joe. There is no heartache like that of losing a child!

Angels in the Snow

Oh, my Kathy!
Today I watched a little girl
making angels in the snow
like a replay of a scene
I watched not long ago.

"Someday," you said,
"I'll be a pretty angel
like my angel in the snow."
But you were just a little girl.
How did you know? How did you know?

Dark Winter

Dark winter came in August to my heart
    to render soul bereft and cold as death.
No matter that it was summer in the world,
    the sun could not dispel dark winter's icy breath.

A light went out and darkness filled my soul.
    Oh, life should leave 'ere one should suffer so.
But life flowed on through broken, frozen heart,
    though I would swear twas naught but ice and snow.

So I did live in darkness for a time
    and still dark winter haunts me in the fall.
Heat of dog-day summers are a sign
    dark winter soon will pay my heart a call.

A Lesson Learned

When I was young I felt so strong!
Why was I then so sure
that I could take whate'er life held?
Through faith I would endure.

No pain would be too sharp to take.
All hardship I could bear.
I would offer up in sacrifice
my pain and loss through prayer.

But now my child is gone from me
and I begin to see:
I am not strong as Jesus was:
Oh, take this cup from me.

Bittersweet

I walk deserted beaches in my mind.
The wind-swept dunes are cold beneath my feet
and the sun, though shining brightly in the sky
provides no warmth on walks so bittersweet.

The beaches of my past were golden, warm;
children, love and laughter all entwined.
There is nothing now where babes once laughed and played
but memory keeps them ever in my mind.

Tears of Winter

Rain falls heavy from the clouds.
Wet leaves hang from trees like winter shrouds.
Oh God, it is my own tear drops I see
and hosts of grieving angels weep with me.
I grieve for life as it flows past like rain-made rivers
    In the street,
forming pools of grief where angel tears and my tears
    often meet.

Where Do You Go?

Where do you go w hen you have no home
    and the streets are ice and snow?
When you're starved and frozen and have no home,
    where can a poor man go?

Does anyone care if you freeze to death?
    Does anyone even know?
Does anyone care if you're hungry and cold
    and have no place to go?

Where do you go when you're covered with snow
    and your heart is full of sorrow,
and you know if you stay outside in the street
    you'll never see tomorrow?

You find the county alms house
    and knock upon the door,
and a sad-eyed lady tells you
    there's no room for any more.

You shuffle away on frozen feet,
    an ugly, pitiful sight,
hoping someone will pity you and
    pay for a room for the night.

Then God takes pity on your frozen soul
    and leads you to the heat
of a vent outside a building and
    at last you warm your feet.

So you are safe for one more night
    from freezing cold and snow.
It doesn't matter that it's not a home.
    Where else can a poor man go?

Where do you go when you have no home
    and your body is broken and bent?
You take your bottle and bundle of rags
    and find a steaming vent.

Note: This poem was inspired by the many cold and homeless people I saw on the streets during the many years I worked in Washington, DC.

Faith and Inspiration

My painting of the Civil War era church
In Kittrell, NC

A Glorious Gift

A child was born in Bethlehem one clear and starry night
while Joseph prayed
and Angels played
on harps of golden light.

When people heard the miracle, from far and wide they came.
Is this the child?
And Mary smiled.
Yes, Jesus is his name.

Out on the desert shepherds heard the herald angels say,
"Go tell the story
of God's great glory.
His son has come this day."

Bring him the children, the sick and the lame,
for Jesus will love them,
and Jesus will heal them,
all in his Father's name.

Then one day on Calvary, the skies were torn asunder.
While lightening flared
and trumpets blared,
the whole earth shook with thunder.

And Jesus gave the glorious gift that only He could give.
And Mary cried
as Jesus died.
Yes, died that we may live.

Communion

The sycamore spreads its leafy arms
  O'er brook and meadow's many charms.
Its here I come to talk with Thee
  in peaceful shade of ancient tree.
I may not hear You when you speak,
  Though You will know its You I seek,
and I, dear Lord, will know You're there
  as You are present everywhere.

My Soul

What does it matter if I am all alone
as long as I can call my soul my own.

It was not sold
for worldly gold
nor given to that faithless lover fame

And I but wait for God this undistinguished soul to claim.

God's Answer

When I was just a little child
    with wonder in my mind,
I searched and searched and questioned,
    but no answers could I find.

So I asked my God in heaven
    Oh, answer, tell me true:
Are my Grandmas up in heaven?
    Are they really there with you?

Then one night He answered me
    as God will always do.
He sent my Mother's Mother
    (I called her Mommy too).

Yes, she came as real as ever
    and sat beside my bed,
with her white hair just as always
    in a bun behind her head.

She sat and rocked and looked at me.
    I saw her smile and sigh.
"I came to tell you not to fret,
    you see, we never die."

No wispy ghost or dream was she.
    "But Mom, you're dead" said I.
She smiled and rocked and answered me.
    "Why child, we never die."

Star Gazing

As I gaze at a midnight, starry sky,
my soul is filled with strange and tender yearning,
and yet with awe and something near to fear.

My soul is beckoned by the universe,
a need to fly among the stars within me burning,
'tis the vessel of my soul that keeps me here.

Again, in light of day, I gaze toward the heavens,
remembering the night's mysterious discerning,
and grieve for that which last night seemed so near.

For man is one with universe and God,
and what seems to be surrealistic yearning
is surely inborn knowledge of another, Godly, sphere.

A Vision

When I was yet a little child, I had a dream one night.
I thought that God was calling me to stand within His light.

The night was filled with music coming from above.
The whole wide world was ringing with the music of God's love.

The clouds began to open up. No sound could then be heard.
A bible lay there open, a symbol of God's word.

Shafts of light came through the clouds and one shone down on me.
There were people in the darkness, but who I could not see.

A voice rang out like thunder from heaven far away.
"I want to tell you now, my child, you're seeing judgment day.

Tell all the people you can find to stand within My light
or when their judgment day is come they'll vanish from My sight."

My heart knows now it was no dream but was a vision clear.
It was God's voice I heard that night, "I'm calling you, my dear."

Days Gone By

Captain Bill and Mary Jane Bailey Griffith.
I believe this was their wedding day

Jenny MacLeod, my great-grandmother and the mother of Captain Bill, was Scottish, a member of the MacLeod Clan from the Isle of Skye. She married Adam Griffith in 1795 when she was fifteen years old and they settled on land in Virginia that had been in the Griffith family for several generations.

Captain Bill, next to youngest of their ten children, became the first steamboat captain on the Coal River when he was only 19 years old. He married Mary Jane Bailey for whom I am named and they lived in what was then Virginia. The city of Charleston, West Virginia, now occupies that farmland. Captain Bill fought for the Confederacy but Mary Jane's brother fought for the Union. This caused her to be accused of being a Union spy so Captain Bill moved his family to his property on Little Brier Creek. Our family still owns a few acres of that land.

Captain Bill

In the early twilight
when the river seems so still,
I can hear a steamboat comin'
and I know it's Captain Bill.

The boys are all a shoutin'
"Steamboat 'round the bend."
I can hear the whistle blowin',
see the smoke upon the wind.

Then Captain Bill is callin'
"I'm home, Miss Mary Jane,"
and I'm runnin' for the river.
The Captain's home again!

He steps down on the levee,
Doffs his hat and takes a bow.
The he has me in a bear hug.
Oh, the captain's home – for now.

I know, of course, he will not stay;
the river has first claim;
but one day he will shout again,
"I'm home, Miss Mary Jane."

Ballad of Jenny MacLeod

Oh, Jenny came from Scotland in a castle by the sea,
    but Jenny left it all behind and came away with me.
She left the purple heather growing by the river Dee
    and she left the old stone castle where the river meets the sea.

Oh, Jenny, my Jenny, she nevermore shall see
    the purple heather blooming down beside the river Dee.

I brought her to the mountains and built a cabin there.
    We picked the mountain laurel and I pinned it in her hair.
Yet in the early twilight when the doves begin to call,
    I see her blue eyes clouded and I see a teardrop fall.

Oh, Jenny, my Jenny, she nevermore shall see
    the purple heather blooming down beside the river Dee.

Jenny's sweet lips are not laughing and her harp sits by the door,
    for Jenny's missing Scotland and the heather on the moor.
She longs for skirling bagpipes and to see that stony keep,
    to see the craggy mountains and to smell the heather sweet.

Oh, Jenny, my Jenny, she nevermore shall see
    the purple heather blooming down beside the river Dee.

I know how much she longs to walk beside the river Dee,
    but Jenny chose to leave it all and now must bide with me.
Now soon again will come the spring; we'll see the bluebirds fly.
    Then Jenny's voice will lift in song; and I shall love her 'til I die.

But Jenny, my Jenny, she nevermore shall see
    the purple heather blooming down beside the river Dee.

Captain bill was very proud of being a Confederate soldier and when he was old he had his picture taken for posterity with his old musket loader and wearing the coat of his Confederate uniform.

When I was a child we heard many stories of the civil war. My father had been very close to Captain Bill, his grandfather, and knew all his war stories. Captain Bill was not an officer but he was always called Captain because he was a steamboat captain before the war and for a time afterward, before the railroads came to make moving coal and timber easier.

The Welsh people have always been gifted story tellers and Daddy was no different. He loved to tell the stories which had been told to him by Captain Bill. The poem about the brothers was inspired by those stories and by my Great Grandmother, Mary Jane's story. Although she was married to Captain Bill who was a confederate, her brother was in the Union army and died at Gettysburg. Many families were split in this way and those sad stories inspired some of my poems. Incidentally, Captain Bill never spoke to his best friend again because he had fought for the North. The friend would come to visit and they would sit in the rocking chairs by the fireplace in the parlor, but Captain Bill would never acknowledge him. When someone reminded him that this man had been his good friend, he said, "I know the damned Yankee," and that was that.

Johnny and His Brother

The brothers said their fond farewells
    and bravely they set forth.
Young Johnny turned toward the south,
    his brother to the north.

Their Mother railed against this war
    where brother must fight brother.
"Oh, my sons," were here last words,
    "do not shoot each other."

They each had made great effort
    not to think about the other,
until the battle of Bull Run
    when Johnny faced his brother.

The battle was still raging
    But for Johnny it was done.
An old man touched his shoulder,
    "What is the matter, son?"

"I cannot fire my rifle, sir,
    My brother wears the blue."
"You have to fire your rifle, son,
    they're firing theirs at you."

But Johnny saw his brother's face
    across the battle ground.
He knew his brother saw him too
    and would not fire his round.

When the battle was all over
    They knew the south had won.
Smoke hung thick upon the air
    and hid the setting sun.

Across the line the brother lay
    his blue all stained with red.
Young John was still, he did not move
    for Johnny Reb was dead.

The old man sat beneath a tree
    to write about the fight.
He recalled that conversation
    and knew what he would write.

With tears upon his weathered cheek
    he wrote the dead boys' mother.
One thing I feel that you should know:
    they did not kill each other.

Homecoming

She sat beneath the old Oak tree, her sewing on her knees.
The summer breeze was gentle in her hair.
She did not see the old plantation, nor the blossoms on the trees.
She was dreaming when he came and found her there.

It seemed a dream came true as he knelt beside her chair
and kissed away the tear drops from her eyes.
The dream was not to be for long, but he was there
for one sweet moment of their lives.

He stood resplendent in his grays, his sword hung by his side,
but within their hearts and souls they wept,
for they knew the south they loved so well had died,
and the flower of southern youth already slept.

But he must return to battle for he loved his southern home
and a little hope still lived within his heart.
So he said goodbye and left her in the garden all alone.
They vowed this was the last time they would part.

Again she sat and waited in the garden – the war was
almost done.
She was thinking of that gentle man in gray.
No matter that the south was now in ashes nor that the
north had won,
for he was coming home to her this day.

She didn't see the ruined plantation, or the weeds beside
her chair.
She was seeing him without the southern gray.
She was dreaming when he came and found her there,
and she knew at last he had come home to stay.

Robert Wore the Gray

When Robert went away to war,
    a lad of twenty-one,
his hopes were high he would be home
    before the year was done.

But Robert fought all summer
    and then the winter came.
The boys were cold and hungry
    but they fought on just the same.

Then spring came round
    and summer too.
It seemed to them forever
    they had fought the northern blue.

They fought the battle of Bull Run
    and won – and won again.
And if they finally lost the war,
    then Rob was not to blame.

For he had fought on valiantly
    beside his gray-clad friends
until the south was on its knees,
    the war was at its end.

Just before the signing
    that would end this useless war,
Rob's world was shattered by a shell
    and Rob would walk no more.

He came home on a stretcher
    but his Mother, too, was brave.
"Be glad, my son, you're safe at home.
    The south could not be saved.

"Oh, son, it does not matter
    that we did not win the day.
You did your best with all the rest
    who wore the southern gray.

"And, son, it does not matter
    that you cannot walk today,
for you will walk tomorrow.
    I know because we'll pray."

Dreams and Fantasy

My painting, Wetlands at Sunrise

Oh, Give Me a Ship

Oh, give me a ship with pure white sails
    and a plane with gossamer wings.
Then give me a hammer and golden nails
    to build me a harp that sings.

I'll sail away on my sailing ship
    to some enchanted land,
or fly to the moon in my aeroplane
    to play in the golden sand.

Perhaps I'll sail out to Valhalla
    in my ship with the pure white sails
and listen while myriad heroes
    enthrall me with splendid tales.

Then surely I'll fly to Olympus
    to visit the pantheon there.
I'll take old Zeus for an aeroplane ride,
    and many a secret we'll share.

And if Valhalla is empty of souls
    and the gods of Olympus all gone,
I'll sit myself down with my magical harp
    And sing of that once mighty throng.

Oh, I'll sail on my ship and fly in my plane
    and see what tomorrow brings.
And I'll never be lonely as long as I have
    my harp with the magical strings.

Where Are All the Leprechauns?

Where are all the leprechauns
    and elves and gnomes and such?
No one ever sees them now.
    How then did we lose touch?

Has the world become too modern?
    Are people now too crass
to see the little people
    in trees or meadow grass?

Perhaps we drove them all away
    to live in other places.
Or maybe no one stops to look
    for tiny elvin faces.

Would that they are not gone away
    or perished from the wood.
Oh, let them still be playing there
    with Little John and Robin Hood.

For someday I must take the time
    to rest in quiet bowers;
to search for that sweet fairyland;
    to stop and smell the flowers.

Perhaps I'll find them living still
    in tree or meadow grass
if I but take the time to see
    before my hour has passed.

Oh, make me then a little child
    with eyes that really look
for flowers and elves and leprechauns
    in every shady nook.

My Soul Wings Free

Sometimes in the night my soul wings free
and I go wherever I wish to be.

I fly over valleys of lush green grass
or watch by the ocean as sailing ships pass.

The sails are like wings in pale moonlight,
misty and fading, lost souls in the night.

My soul is reminded that it must fly on.
My prison awaits in the cold gray dawn.

For the soul cannot fly in its body of clay
which renders me earthbound during the day.

But, oh, when my soul wings free in the night
I remember that someday I'll reach a new height.

Then never again will my soul be earthbound,
and I'll fly o'er the clouds where true joy is found

The Fairy Glen

Down in the glen,
late at night . . .
down in the deep, green hollow,
I hear the lilt of fairy pipes.
Oh, how I long to follow!

The glen is haunted,
old folks say . . .
and eerie tales they tell
of those who dare where fairies play
and cast their magic spell.

And yet they call me
to the glen . . .
down in the deep, green hollow.
I know enchantment waits for me
if I were just to follow!

Down to the glen
they lure me . . .
with promise of delight.
And sure they'll steal my heart and soul
some dark, enchanted night.

A Cowboy's Dream

I spent my youth in the Texas sun
with a hat for shade and an old six-gun.
Most of the time I was on the run
and I never knew when the west was won.

I worked sometimes as a poor cowhand
down in Texas by the Rio Grande.
At night I slept with a gun in my hand
beneath the stars on the burning sand.

Across the river in an old canteen
I could hear the Caballeros sing,
with two guitars and a tambourine,
of a Mexican girl and a Mexican dream.

A Mexican girl with a tambourine
became this cowboy's special dream
as I listened to those cowhands sing.
And I yearned to be in that old canteen.

So I crossed the river at El Paso
and found my dream in Mexico:
a dark-eyed girl who likes to sing
with two guitars and a tambourine.

I still punch cattle in the burning sun
with a hat for shade and an old six-gun.
But I spend my nights in that old canteen
with my dark-eyed girl and her tambourine.

I no longer sleep beneath the stars
so I traded my pack for an old guitar
and I've never looked back at El Paso
across the river from Mexico.

Moods and Feelings

Butterflies

Winter Birds

Winter birds fly by,
uncertain forms against the gray October sky,
for they, like I, grasp nothing solid on this earth
and only God can know the birds' true worth.

Winter birds fly by
and here am I,
fading like those pale, illusive wings against the sky.

Race With The Stars

Stars swirl
in a midnight sky
over Monte Carlo.
The sea below
is obsidian.

Stars whirl
and we can fly.
Around and down we go.
The world we know
is our meridian.

Stars swirl
as we race madly by.
Laughter dies upon the wind
as we descend
into oblivion.

Do Not Miss the Morning

Come, come, come.
Do not miss the morning sun.
See it peeps above the mountain,
like a lovely golden fountain.

Hear? The birds are all a'twitter
and the lake begins to glitter
as the sun sends out his rays.
Do not miss these golden days.

Rise, rise, rise.
You must see the morning skies.
Do not be a sleepy head.
You must see: the skies are red.

Soon the sun will be up high
burning in the noon-day sky.
Come enjoy the morning dew.
God has put it there for you.

Feelings

Some days are darkness,
    and steady rainfall,
plaintive and gray
    as the mourning dove's call.

Some days are heavy,
    weighing me down,
stifling and dark
    like a black, velvet gown.

But some days are made of
    crystal blue light,
filling my senses
    with wondrous delight.

And some days are golden,
    sparkling and new,
like the sun in the morning
    when I am with you.

Ribbons

Ribbons of road and rolling green hills
    and valleys deep and wide,
and left behind with the lights of the town
    are the tears I've already cried.

Ribbons of cloud and blue summer skies,
    and beaches washed clean with the tide,
but left behind is the love I once knew
    and my tears have already dried.

Ribbons of rainbow and roses in bloom,
    and gone are the days when I sighed,
for now I've found a new life and love
    and forgotten the tears that I cried.

Irish Tears

Kelli's Shamrocks

An American of Irish descent may be several generations removed from the old country but Ireland remains forever in his heart. This love of Ireland and the turmoil in Ireland in the 1970's and 1980's touched the heart of many Irish Americans and inspired the following poems.

Weep With Me was written in 1981 when Bobby Sands and several other Irish republicans went on a hunger strike in jail. Shortly after I wrote the poem Bobby died of starvation. He did gain some concessions for Ireland but only he could judge whether his sacrifice was worth it.

Weep With Me

Weep with me my children, let me hear the banshee's wail.
Weep you wives and lovers for the boys who starve in jail.
Weep for dear old Ireland, for the IRA shall fail.

Weep you babes in cradles for your father's bloody hands.
Weep for all the useless death; and weep for Bobby Sands
Then weep again for Ireland, for divided it still stands.

Weep you sons and daughters for the Irish lives you take.
Weep you gray-haired Mothers, weep for thine own sake.
Weep you bloody Ireland: 'tis grief, 'tis grief you make.

Call of the Sea

I hear a distant drummer
and a lilting piper's tune.
I tilt my head
and listen.
Ah, 'twas naught but Mollie's loom!

My ale is warm and soothing,
my bread fresh baked today.
But what is that?
I listen.
Ah, 'twas but the bairns at play!

I smell the salty sea wind
and hear the roar of surf.
I tilt my head
And listen.
Ah, 'twas just the blazing turf!

Oh, Mollie, can't you hear it?
The call of distant sea?
She tilts her head
And listens.
Nay, 'tis wind off Innisfree!

Don't look so sad, my Mollie.
You know my blood's salt brine.
Its siren call does
haunt me,
but, Moll, my heart is thine!

Yet down the track I follow
that drum and piper's tune.
Is that a sob
behind me?
Nay, 'tis naught but Mollie's loom!

An Irish Story

Gnarled fingers clutched a knobby, hand-made cane.
    An old tweed cap perched on his balding head.
Craggy features, creased and lined, betrayed his age,
    and revealed the troubled life which he had led.

Toil and poverty had marked their places all too well,
    and love – for he had been a family man of sorts.
But adventure could no longer light the eyes
    red now from sharing countless pints with old cohorts.

Sometimes a hint of twinkle would return,
    for a little ale can cause a man to put aside
all thought of hardship and remember only good.
    Indeed, the rich man's life most time he would deride.

But today his was a strictly sober mien
    as he entered that dark room behind the local pub.
Well he knew the men for he had once been just like them,
    But time had taught him many truths – ah, there's the rub.

What seemed now to him a dark and sinister milieu
    had once caused his eager, youthful heart to wildly race.
Long moments now the men around the table stared at him,
    as the glow of stubby cigarettes revealed each face.

Then they went on as though the old man were not there.
　　(They knew he'd never give their plans away.)
"Go 'way, old man," the nearest one remarked.
　　"Don't preach at us for you have had your day.

Don't tell us that we fight for hopeless cause,
　　nor tell us that you think we cannot win.
We've more and better weapons now, old man.
　　And we are stronger, braver men."

He could not even laugh at their conceit,
　　but wept for men long gone who'd said the same.
"Your cause is lost but that isn't my concern.
　　What matters is the awful grief and shame

Of men who fight and kill their own for just a dream.
　　What difference who has power or who does reign?
For freedom's in the heart – a state of mind.
　　And tyranny though slain, is always born again."

But the boys went on with planning daring deeds,
　　while stale smoke joined with the whiskey fumes,
and the crackling fire licked shadows on the sooty walls.
　　(He had seen the same hard faces in a hundred other rooms.)

Yet one face among the others swam before his saddened eyes
　　as the old man turned and left, his head bowed low.
He saw his boy, Liam, as he had done a thousand times,
　　Singing in the church choir not so very long ago.

The boys then left to carry out their last big plan,
　　and soon the old man leaned again on gnarled cane.
The choir was singing softly but the old man's head bowed low,
　　for he'd never hear his Liam lift his voice in song again.

★ 99 ★

Take Me Home, Macushla

Oh, take me home, Macushla, to the place where I was born
    in that cottage in Kilkenney on a lovely, misty morn;
one more son of Ireland who loved her next to God;
    two more hands to work and fight to free the dear auld sod.

What, you would deny me this? Whence all those years of toil?
    'Tis all I've ever asked of thee – to rest on Irish soil.
You made me leave my Ireland. Oh God, it was not I.
    Do not weep, Macushla, but 'tis there that I must die.

Oh, take me back, Macushla, love, where first these eyes did see.
    Let them behold just one more time that land so dear to me.
Oh, take me home, Macushla, love, to where I first drew breath.
    I gave you all I had to give, now give me this in death.

Please take me home, Macushla, across the Irish sea.
    For though my Ireland needed me, I gave my life to thee.
Now leave me in the meadow where the dew is soft and sweet.
    And there I'll wait, Macushla, 'til again we two shall meet.

Shadows in the Canyons

My painting, Tepees at Dawn, painted from my imagination

I lived for several years in Ruidoso, New Mexico in the Sierra Blanca Mountains. The Ruidoso River ran through a cool, dark canyon and it was easy to imagine the Indians as they might have been when they were first settled in those mountains after they were defeated. Apaches still live on that New Mexico Reservation and many of them bear the famous name of Geronimo. They now own and run the beautiful Inn of the Mountain Gods and Casino, and Ski Apache.

Sierra Blanca

Sierra Blanca, sacred mountain
hovers o'er the white man's town
and the river rushes down
with a lonely secret sound.

Indian gods still linger darkly
on that sacred, frozen ground
in eternal conversation
with the river rushing down.

The mountain waits there brooding
in a silence quite profound,
enduring with the ancient gods
and the river rushing down.

Enchanted Canyon

I see them in the shadows
    of the Ponderosa pines
in Ruidoso Canyon
    where the sun so seldom shines.

Ah, those Indian braves of yesterday,
    they evermore shall dwell
in that dark, enchanted canyon
    under ancient Indian spell.

I hear their voices in the wind,
    soft whispers in the trees,
and I hear their cautious footsteps
    in the rustle of the leaves.

Ah, those Indian braves of yesterday,
    'twas freedom that they sought.
Now they're planning phantom battles
    which never can be fought.

I feel their teardrops falling
    with the gentle summer rain,
joining with the river
    in its endless, sad refrain.

And in the misty canyon,
    frail spirits can be seen
where Indian braves of yesterday
    forever live their dream.

An Indian's Vision

An Indian stood on the mountain top,
    his arms stretched toward the sky.
He could not feel the snow and ice,
    nor hear the eagle's cry.

He would not eat, nor would he drink
    until a vision came
to help him save his people
    who were starving on the plain.

The north wind whistled 'round him,
    the black wolf howled his name.
But he heard no sound around him,
    nor freezing, felt the pain.

Then in the mists he saw the plain,
    shimmering and green
and herds of shaggy buffalo
    beside a flowing spring.

A smile played on his marble face
    as hope was kindled there.
Still silently he waited
    remembering his prayer.

The vision changed to horror,
    his hope to disbelief.
The brief smile left his frozen lips,
    his eyes were pools of grief.

This could not be, yet it was true,
    the spirits had revealed
the end of all he loved so well:
    the Redman's fate was sealed.

The white man came like swarms of flies
    across the misty plain,
and bullets fell upon the tribes
    like drops of frozen rain.

Now he saw within the mist,
    the thundering herd was dead.
They lay like blots upon the plain.
    His heart was filled with dread.

The mists moved on the icy wind.
    The brave had had his dream.
He sat immobile as a stone
    and wept for what he'd seen.

His eyes now saw the snow and ice.
    He felt the freezing wind.
Now the eagle called his name
    and he knew it was the end.

The wind became the eerie call
    of braves gone on before.
Then he was one with mother earth.
    The Indian was no more.

Cree Meadows

Mist rises on Cree Meadows
    in the early light of dawn
as the sun appears all golden on the hill.

The Ruidoso river
    where the speckled trout will spawn
slips by the sleeping wigwams. All is still.

Thin wisps of smoke curl upward
    from fires banked for the night.
Peace is on the meadows everywhere.

Then a bird begins to sing
    as day replaces night,
and one lone voice begins to chant a plaintive prayer.

But suddenly the sun is high,
    the meadows bathed in light.
The camp was but a vision or a dream.

Cree Meadows is still a meadow
    but the Indians are not there.
And the speckled trout leaps lonely in the stream.

For The Child
in All of Us

Joseph Ullery, one of my seven perfect great-grandchildren.

Mary Ann Mouse

Mary Ann Mouse lived in a house
    on Brambleberry Lane.
She was a good girl, but her hair wouldn't curl.
    Indeed she was really quite plain.

Her sister, Nancy, was really quite fancy
    and pretty as could be.
All the young mice thought she was nice
    but Nancy was fancy-free.

She vowed not to marry Tom Dick or Harry
    but wait for riches and fame.
With her nose in the air, and bows in her hair,
    she played a waiting game.

But Mary was smart and had a warm heart.
    The boys liked her as a friend.
Though sister Nancy was really quite fancy,
    it was Mary who won in the end.

She married a mouse who had a huge house
    and loved her sweet disposition.
For Nan it's too late, she continues to wait,
    though now she is full of contrition.

High Topped Adidas

Ol' Ricky Racoon wanted shoes very badly
but 'coons don't wear shoes - he acknowledged that gladly.

Still, he waited and hoped for someone to discard
their old tennis shoes -- and the waiting was hard!

After waiting and waiting, he finally found
just what he had dreamed of, right on the ground.

They lay in a box, those high-topped adidas,
close by the trash where he ate his fajitas.

He put them both on, two feet in each one,
but to his chagrin, he could no longer run.

So proudly he took them and stored them away
where he could feast his eyes on them every day.

For any Raccoon might feast on fajitas
but none other he knew had high-topped adidas.

A Lesson for Harriet

Down on the farm in a little red barn lived Harriet the little
red hen.
Hubert the horse lived there, of course, and up in the loft
lived a wren.

Pierre le Pig, who was really quite big, lived downwind in
a sty.
While Calvin C. Cat stayed sleek and fat for he lived in the
house nearby.

Now Harriet would lay an egg every day and then go out
for a snack.
The egg would lie there, uncovered and bare, and everyone
noticed that fact.

"You'd better stay here and guard that, my dear," said Rabbit
who lived in a box,
"for that egg, nice and brown, will be eaten if found, by
Rennie the Renegade Fox."

"Ha," said Ms. Hen, I never have been afraid of anything
here."
"Well," said Pierre, "You'd better take care, for Rennie is
speedy I hear."

You're just being silly. It's much too chilly for Fox to come out of his lair.
He'll never get me and as you can see, I'm not that easy to scare."

So she put on her bonnet with red ribbons on it and went out walking at dawn.
She was looking for seeds among the tall weeds just at the edge of the lawn.

Behind some big rocks lurked Rennie the Fox, waiting to pounce on Ms. Hen.
But high in the barn, the sound of alarm was given by Winnie the Wren.

Ms. Hen didn't hear, but Hubert was near so he neighed as loud as he could.
Ms. Hen heard the whinny and so did old Rennie and he disappeared in the wood.

"Thanks," said the Hen to Winnie the Wren." "You saved both me and my egg.
For if you hadn't watched, I would have been foxed. Rennie's a real renegade."

With a toss of her head, Ms. Harriet said, "That was a good lesson for me."
Then when they'd all shout, "You'd better watch out," Ms. Hen would instantly flee.

Traveling

Sammy the snail always traveled by rail
    wherever he would go,
though he would go by air if he had the fare
    for snails are notoriously slow.

His friend the goat preferred to float
    around in a big balloon.
But Sammy the snail was afraid it would fail
    and carry him up to the moon.

I might like to sail, said Sammy the snail
    but it limits where you can go.
An automobile said Sonny the seal
    is great in rain or snow.

If I had snow, said Caroline crow,
     I'd get myself a ski.
Skis are too big, said Pierre the pig
     just jump like Freddy the Flea.

He does move quickly, but I am too sickly,
     and cannot jump so far,
said Sammy the snail who traveled by rail,
     but someday I may get a car.

You could, said the flea, or travel like me
     on the back of an old shaggy dog.
Oh well, said the snail, I'll stick to the rail
     Unless I grow legs, then I'll jog.

Sweet William's Disgrace

The Hollyhocks stood by the garden gate
    like soldiers, straight and tall,
while Raggedy Sailors stood their watch
    along the garden wall.

The Iris held their purple flags
    beside the old brick walk,
and Old Maids in their bright red hats
    had ceased their silly talk.

The Four O'Clocks had closed their eyes
    against the bright sunshine
but Portulaca didn't care –
    it was siesta time.

The Bleeding Heart was weeping in her
    corner in the shade,
and the Bachelor's Buttons halted
    their perennial parade.

The Trumpet vine had changed his tune
    from reveille to taps,
while Dandelions stopped roaring and
    doffed their yellow caps.

Snapdragon was not snapping –
    he was paralyzed with shock.
The Violets were hiding out
    behind the purple Stock.

The purple velvet Pansy raised her
    sad-eyed face and said:
"Alas, our poor Sweet William
    has fallen out of bed."

The Robin in the Pear Tree
    could see poor Will's disgrace,
so he picked him up quite gently and
    set him back in place.

Sweet William was so happy
    to be saved from misery,
he stood at full attention
    with a smile for all to see.

Now all the gloom has vanished from
    the garden by the wall,
and no one will ever mention
    Sweet William's tragic fall.

Benny The Bear And Ling Ling

Benny the bear
sat on a chair
    in little Shawna's bedroom.
Nearby on the floor
sat quite a few more
    toys awaiting a full moon.

For when moon was bright,
then throughout the night
    they all would dance and sing.
And Benny the Bear
always took care
    to dance with the Panda, Ling Ling.

When Shawna would sleep
and the full moon would peep
    over the window sill,
That's when they came out
and danced all about
    'til dawn came over the hill.

One night some slight noise
made by the toys
    caused Shawna to wake in surprise
So just by pure chance
she saw them all dance.
    She couldn't believe her own eyes.

They stopped right away
and there they all lay.
    She thought it had all been a dream.
But Benny the Bear
was not in his chair.
    He sat on the table with Ling Ling.

That's how Shawna knew
that it was all true.
    She had seen them all dance and sing.
She put them in place
then saw Benny's face
    and knew poor Benny loved Ling Ling.

Now Ling Ling the bear
sits on the same chair,
    hand in hand with her Benny.
They're happy again.
You should see Benny's grin!
    And Shawna's as happy as any.

Crocodile Tears

Way down south at the edge of the swamp
    lived Freddy the little green frog.
And quite nearby lived a crocodile
    beneath a hollow log.

Now the frog liked to lie
    on that log in the sun,
but when Croc would come out,
    old Freddy would run.

One day Freddy slipped
    and fell in the swamp.
He knew Croc could eat him
    in just one chomp.

Freddy was frightened –
    he thought he was dead!
But Croc didn't eat him,
    he saved him instead.

I want to be friends
    said that old Crocodile,
putting frog on the log
    with a crocodile smile.

But frog didn't trust him
    and ran far away.
Perhaps he was right –
    we don't know to this day.

Croc swore he was saddened
    by Freddy Frog's fears,
and he cried the very first
    crocodile tears.

Jehosephat the Cat

Jehosephat was a big black cat
    who thought he was really tough.
He liked to chase rats and silly blind bats
    and generally make their lives rough.

But one day a dog named Phineous Phogg
    came into the barnyard to play.
He chased that old cat named Jehosephat
    around and around all day.

'Til he tired of his play and wandered away
    and left the old cat to his rest.
Now cat knows he's not as tough as he thought,
    but he still is the barnyard pest.

Does a Bear Need Money?

If you were a bear with fuzzy black hair
    and didn't have any money,
would you worry a lot? I think you would not.
    I'm sure you would think it was funny.

For a big old bear with fuzzy black hair
    who lived in a big hollow tree,
would never need money – bears only eat honey.
    They don't buy it, they take it you see.

Ribbet

Freddie the little green frog
left his home by the old hollow log
for beneath the log lived a crocodile
in his slithery, slathery, domicile.

Fred was afraid of that crocodile
with his watery, toothy, crocodile smile,
so he ran far away 'til he came to a pond
and a little house beneath a fern frond.

The house was shady and really quite damp
and its only light was a firefly lamp.
But Freddie loved to be wet and he loved to be cool
so he often swam in the big cool pool.

Now Fred was a bachelor and liked it that way
so he could go fishing every day
and have his friends in for a little card game.
He just knew a wife would gripe and complain.

One day as he floated around on the pond
and fanned himself with a wet fern frond,
he spied on a lily pad quite nearby
a pretty girl frog who winked her eye.

Freddie the frog fell in love on the spot.
His plans to stay single were promptly forgot.
His love for Miss Frog he made quite plain,
but it seemed his courting would be in vain.

Miss Frog was a flirt but she was not ready
to settle down with someone like Freddie.
But Freddie would win her hand he insisted.
So in spite of her protests, Freddie persisted.

One summer night when the full moon was shining,
he said to himself "Enough of this pining."
He got out his guitar to sing a love song,
and to give him courage, his friends went along.

They serenaded Miss Frog in the pale moonlight
and she fell in love that very same night.
Now Fred and Miss Frog are happily wed.
She thinks no one sings as well as her Fred.

Now they swim all the time in the cool, green pond
while he fans his wife with a green fern frond.
You can walk by the pond any night of your choice
and you'll hear Freddie sing in his deep basso voice . . . .

Ribbet…Ribbet…Ribbet.

Shawna Banona

Shawna Banona, puddin' and pie.
The apple of her pappy's eye.

Shawna Banona and Duke the dog
and Pappy love to run and jog.

Shawna Banona, sugar and spice.
Grandma loves her, naughty or nice.

Shawna Banona, run and play.
You're mommy's when you don't obey.

Squirrel, Squirrel

Squirrel, squirrel in the tree,
why are you afraid of me?
I won't hurt you – no not I.
Cross my heart and hope to die.

Squirrel, squirrel in the tree,
you wave your bushy tail at me,
but I can't tempt you to come down
though I leave nuts upon the ground.

Squirrel, squirrel in the tree,
please come down and play with me.
A friend is all I want to be
and I would always leave you free.